MW00929903

THIS BOOK BELONGS TO:

Made in the USA
Monee, IL
07 March 2021

62135040R00066